written by Richard Brightfield

Table of Contents | Page

# Exploring Nature With a Camera

How does a hummingbird fly? How does a rose open? How does a jaguar leap?

One of the best ways to study the world around you is with a camera. Going out to take pictures helps you focus on your surroundings. Photography also helps you develop respect for the creatures in your world. It allows you to remember what you have seen. Pictures may show you things your eyes might not have noticed.

Photography is a useful tool for *naturalists*. They are people who study nature. Some naturalists are professional scientists. Others explore living things as a hobby. For some bird watchers, a camera is as important as a pair of binoculars.

In the past, amateur naturalists often hunted the animals in their collection and stuffed them for display. People on safari, for example, would travel to different parts of Africa to shoot as many wild animals as they could! Today, photo safaris have largely replaced hunting. Eager photographers drive miles into conservation parks to "shoot"—with a camera. They photograph rare animals like cheetahs. Showing off the pictures back home is a much greater thrill when you know that your subject is still alive.

If you were to go on a photo safari in Africa, you would probably take a lot of equipment. Yet even with a simple camera, you can learn about nature in a local park, wildlife preserve, forest, or swamp.

# Stop the Action!

The camera can help you see things that move too fast or too slowly for your eyes to catch. Like airplane propellers, the legs of a galloping horse are a blur when seen with the unaided eye.

Leland Stanford, former governor of California, once made a bet with a friend during a horse race. Stanford claimed that as a horse galloped, there were moments when it lifted all four hooves off the ground. His friend thought that was impossible. Stanford hired Eadweard Muybridge, an English inventor and photographer, to prove his point. Five years later, Muybridge settled the bet. Beside a race track, he placed 24 cameras twelve inches apart. As the horse galloped past, each camera took a very fast picture. Sure enough, in one image, all four hooves were in the air!

How did Muybridge get his pictures to look so still and sharp? Every camera has a device called a shutter. It opens and closes to let light into the camera. If the subject moves while the shutter is open, the image will look blurred. Muybridge solved the problem by inventing a shutter that would open and close in 1/1000th of a second! The horse hardly moves any distance in such a tiny fraction of time.

Today, electronic shutters on special cameras may take a picture in one–millionth of a second. An ordinary camera, by contrast, has a shutter speed of about 1/50th of a second. This might sound very fast. Yet if your camera's "click" scares a squirrel as you snap its picture, you will find out just how fast animals can get out of the frame!

One easy way to avoid blurry images is to photograph things that move very slowly. Many photographers have a passion for photographing plant life. Without wind, these things tend to stay still.

Photographers know that if they leave the shutter open longer, they will get a richer, more detailed photograph. They might also use a tripod, a camera stand with three legs. The tripod keeps the camera steady while the shutter is open—much steadier than photographers could hold it with their hands alone.

What if you enjoy taking pictures of animals in their natural habitat? What if you just have to have a photograph of that jaguar—or that graceful deer?

One way to get close to a wild animal is to build a *blind*. This is a shelter in which a photographer can hide from an animal's view. To use a blind, you have to know just where your subject is going to appear. In a desert, for example, animals will often return to the same stream or watering hole. Photographers will build blinds nearby to shoot the animals when they come to drink.

Having the right gear helps, too. All cameras have a lens. A lens is a thick piece of glass that works like a magnifying glass. A *telephoto lens* turns a camera into a telescope. With it, you could be waiting hundreds of feet away. Yet, in your picture, the jaguar will look close enough to touch.

To take a good photograph, a photographer needs to make sure that enough light enters the shutter. In a traditional camera, light "exposes" the image as it reacts with chemicals in the film. Then the film is developed into slides or is printed on paper. Yet if light is needed, how would a photographer capture an animal in flight—or in the dark? Here is an interesting case.

About one million bats live in Carlsbad Caverns, in New Mexico. The Caverns, a national monument, are famous for these bats. Like all bats, these bats are nocturnal. This means they are active at night and sleep during the day.

Zoologists were puzzled by the bats in Carlsbad Caverns. These bats lack a piece of skin stretched between the hind legs that allow other bats to steer while in flight. How did the Carlsbad bats fly without it?

A photo that showed the bats in flight was needed. In the 1930s, Harold E. Edgerton solved the problem of how to catch the bats on film. He invented a *strobe light,* a light that flashes on and off very quickly. He set up his camera and strobe lights at the entrance to the cavern and photographed the bats as they flew out in great numbers at twilight to feed. His high-speed pictures showed that the bats did have a piece of skin, or membrane, that slid out along their tails to help them steer. When the bats weren't in flight, the skin was curled up. This was why no one had noticed it before.

Edgerton's strobe light helped him photograph outdoors at night. Even with a flash, though, you might be surprised at how dark your own pictures may come out when you shoot indoors.

# The Mystery of Flight

Of all nature's creatures, birds are among the most interesting and beautiful. Birds in flight make a dramatic photograph. If the picture blurs a bit, that may suggest the bird's graceful movement.

Another way to capture a flying creature is by *panning.* This means tracking the birds with the camera as they fly. The best way is to begin by moving the camera smoothly in the direction the bird is going, by releasing the shutter, and by continuing the motion after the shutter closes. This is similar to a method movie cameras use to follow moving subjects.

One of the greatest challenges of nature photography has been to take sharp pictures of hummingbirds in flight. Hummingbirds hover in mid-air as they sip nectar from flowers with their long tongues. Hummingbirds' wings beat so fast—up to 60 times per second—that even when photographed with a strobe flash at 1/10,000th of a second, their wing tips can still be blurred.

Luckily for photographers, hummingbirds can be lured to feeding stations with a bit of honey water. Although these birds fear people, they do not seem to be bothered by cameras or large equipment such as strobe lights. Photographers can use remote control to snap the picture from a distance. One high-speed camera uses a strobe light that can shoot twelve hundred frames a second. The result is razor-sharp pictures.

It turns out that hummingbirds don't flap their wings like other birds. They fly more like miniature, hovering helicopters. Their wings beat backwards and forwards rather than up and down. Their wings can also turn upside down to allow them to perform tricky maneuvers in mid-air.

Another creature that was once mysterious was the bumblebee. Naturalists used to joke that the reason bumblebees fly is that no one had ever told them they couldn't! Their tiny wings did not seem large enough to support their thick bodies in the air. Only recently have scientist-photographers, such as Stephen Dalton, discovered how they do it.

Bees and other "heavy" insects do not flap their wings. Rather, their wings make figure eight motions in the air about one thousand times per second. These motions act like propellers to lift the bee into the air.

# The Patient Eye

Insects are the most numerous of all living creatures. A *close-up* lens helps when photographing these animals. This lens makes a picture larger than the actual size of the subject. You might be able to photograph a large insect like a butterfly or a dragonfly without special equipment. You will need patience, though, to wait until the insect is still.

Photography can slow down things that are too fast for you to see. Photos can also do the opposite. They can appear to speed up things that move too slowly for you to observe. If you mark the exact spot to place your camera, you can photograph a plant at the same time every day to show a record of its life. You might have seen this method, called *time-lapse photography,* in movies. Before your eyes, roses seem to blossom, apples to ripen, and trees to shoot up toward the sky.

In spring, plants in cooler climates quickly come to life. That can be a good time to photograph a bush or tree every day. If you see a flower that is beginning to blossom, try photographing it every three hours. For a longer project, you might shoot a particular tree every week for a year. Start when its leaves open in the spring and continue until its colors change in autumn.

You might do the same with a whole landscape—even one that has buildings, cars, and people in it. There is no limit to what you can do with photography. One *anthropologist*—a scientist who studies people—has for many years photographed his children once a week to show their growth. You could try photographing your family on a special holiday each year.

There are many things in nature to photograph. The more you learn about the natural world, the more you will care about preserving the wildlife of the planet.

The possibilities of nature photography are endless. Underwater photography is an exciting area of discovery and recreation. You don't have to go scuba diving in the ocean, however, to find new subjects. The local park is filled with natural wonders, if you know how to look for them.

As you can see, photography is a rewarding hobby. Anyone can do it. All you need is a camera and a good eye.